What Can You Be?

Follow along through the alphabet to discover some of the amazing things that any girl can be when she grows up. The world is full of possibilities!

A is for Astronaut

SHE blasts into outer space to explore new worlds. Wow!

B is for Botanist

SHE carefully studies plants to see what makes them grow.

 is for **Chef**

SHE chops, flips, and sizzles to create delicious food for you and me.

D is for Deep Sea Diver

SHE swims with the fish to investigate life on the ocean floor.

E is for Engineer

SHE builds new things and understands how different parts fit together.

F is for Firefighter

SHE fights fires and rescues people from burning buildings.

G is for Gymnast

SHE jumps, flips, and cartwheels to win gold medals in worldwide competitions.

H is for **Hairstylist**

SHE clips, curls, twists, and braids to make others look their best.

I is for Interior Designer

SHE picks out perfect patterns
and comfy couches to make
our homes beautiful.

J **is for Judge**

SHE makes decisions in court to promote justice and fairness for all.

K is for Keyboardist

SHE plays music with her band and performs at rock concerts around the world.

L is for **Librarian**

SHE helps children discover the wonderful world of books.

m is for **Mechanic**

SHE fixes cars, trucks, and even planes to keep them running smoothly and safely.

N is for **Neurosurgeon**

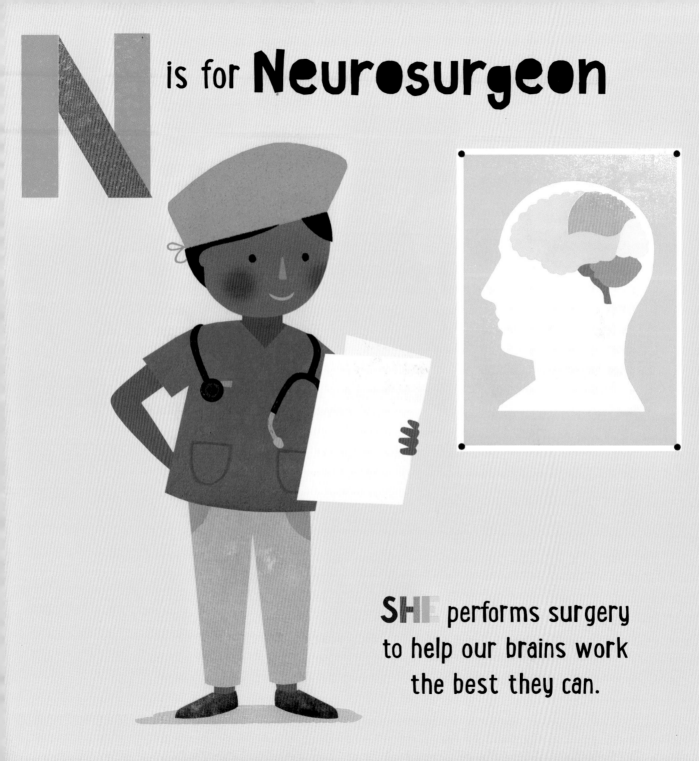

SHE performs surgery to help our brains work the best they can.

is for **Optometrist**

E
F P
T O Z
L R E D
E C F D L
D F C Z P

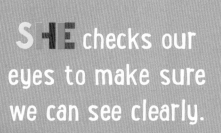

SHE checks our eyes to make sure we can see clearly.

P is for Pilot

SHE flies around the world in her jumbo jet airplane.

Q is for Quantum Physicist

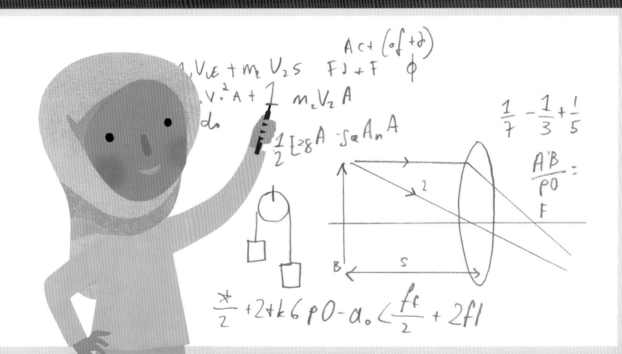

SHE studies atoms, electrons, and other tiny things to understand how our world works.

R is for Referee

SHE knows all the rules and makes sure we play fairly.

S is for Software Engineer

SHE writes code to make computer software and programs.

T is for **Teacher**

SHE teaches us new things so we can make our dreams come true.

U is for UN Ambassador

SHE promotes unity and friendship
with leaders from around the world.

V is for Vice President

SHE works closely with the President and is ready to take charge at a moment's notice.

is for
Writer

SHE uses words to educate
and entertain others with
articles, stories, and poetry.

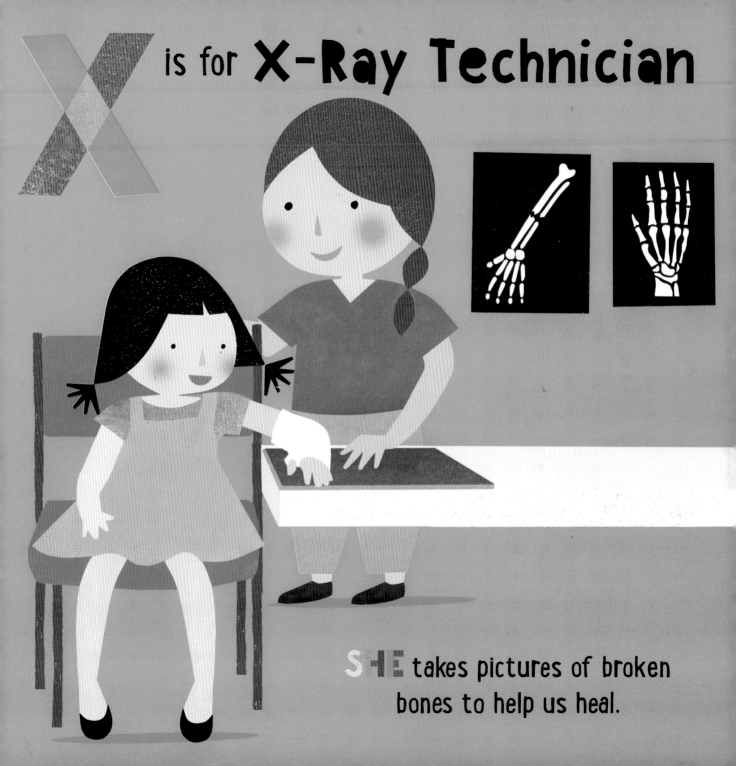

X is for X-Ray Technician

SHE takes pictures of broken bones to help us heal.

Y is for **Yoga Instructor**

SHE teaches people how to move
to make their bodies strong and flexible.

Z is for Zoologist

SHE studies and cares for animals in their native habitats.

A Astronaut **B** Botanist **C** Chef **D** Deep Sea Diver **E** Engineer **F** Firefighter

G H I J K L M

Gymnast Hairstylist Interior Judge Keyboardist Librarian Mechanic
Designer

N O P Q R S

Neurosurgeon

Optometrist

Pilot

Quantum Physicist

Referee

Software Engineer

T U V W X Y Z

T Teacher   **U** UN Ambassador   **V** Vice President   **W** Writer   **X** X-Ray Technician   **Y** Yoga Instructor   **Z** Zoologist

Brimming with creative inspiration, how-to projects, and useful information to enrich your everyday life, Quarto Knows is a favorite destination for those pursuing their interests and passions. Visit our site and dig deeper with our books into your area of interest: Quarto Creates, Quarto Cooks, Quarto Homes, Quarto Lives, Quarto Drives, Quarto Explores, Quarto Gifts, or Quarto Kids.

© 2018 Quarto Publishing Group USA Inc.
Illustrations and text © 2018 Jessie Ford

First published in 2018 by Walter Foster Jr., an imprint of The Quarto Group.
26391 Crown Valley Parkway, Suite 220, Mission Viejo, CA 92691, USA.
T (949) 380-7510 F (949) 380-7575 www.QuartoKnows.com

Walter Foster Jr. titles are also available at discount for retail, wholesale, promotional, and bulk purchase. For details, contact the Special Sales Manager by email at specialsales@quarto.com or by mail at The Quarto Group, Attn: Special Sales Manager, 100 Cummings Center, Suite 265D, Beverly, MA 01915, USA.

ISBN: 978-1-60058-985-0

Digital edition published in 2018
eISBN: 978-1-63322-625-8

Printed in China
10 9 8 7 6 5 4 3 2 1

FSC
www.fsc.org
MIX
Paper from
responsible sources
FSC® C124385